Barbara Kolb
Cloudspin

for Organ

BOOSEY&HAWKES

DISTRIBUTED BY

HAL•LEONARD® CORPORATION

7777 W. BLUEMOUND RD. P.O. BOX 13819 MILWAUKEE, WI 53213

www.boosey.com
www.halleonard.com

Commissioned by the Musart Society
for the Cleveland Museum of Art's 75th anniversary

First performed May 6, 1991 at the Schloßkirche, Bayreuth, Germany by Karel Paukert

Registration by Carson Cooman

COMPOSER'S NOTE

Cloudspin attempts to combine an approach to structure and poetic imagery as related to classifying cloud types. As various terms defining characteristics of clouds also apply to music – suspension, ascending/descending, expansion/contraction, and density, for example – I chose to create a work complementing these atmospheric images.

Cloudspin begins without thematic material or any clear harmonic field, gradually increasing in density through ascending chromatic progressions and rhythmic acceleration. At its peak, measure 33, the situation reverses itself with the upper voices descending while the pedal ascends. A gradual decrease in rhythmic activity occurs to the end, resolving peacefully on a perfect fifth.

—Barbara Kolb

Duration: 5 minutes

dedicated to Karel Paukert

CLOUDSPIN

for Organ

Barbara Kolb

Registration:

1	2	3
I: 8' Flute	I.: 8', 4' Flutes, 8' Principals	I: 8', 4', 2' Foundations, Mutations, Mixture
II: 8', 4' Flutes	II.: 8', 4' Flutes, 2' Principal/Flute, 8' String	II: 8', 4', 2' Foundations, 8', 16' Reeds
	Ped.: 16', 8' Flutes/Principals	II to I
	I to Ped.	I to Ped.
	Box (on II) closed	II to Ped.

M-051-23478-3

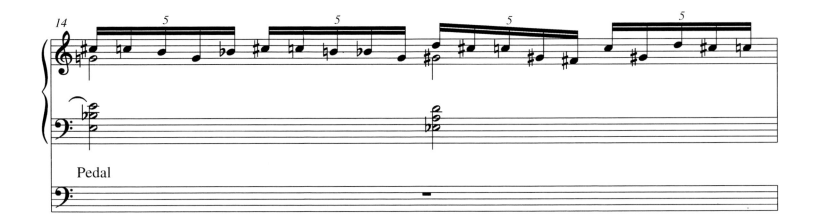

4

gradually open box

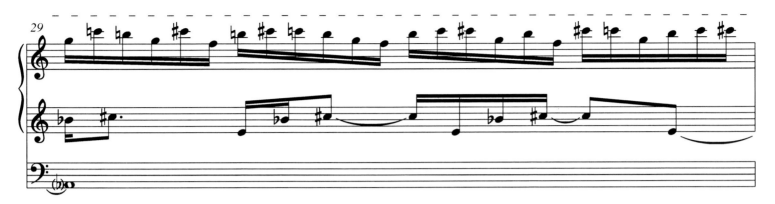

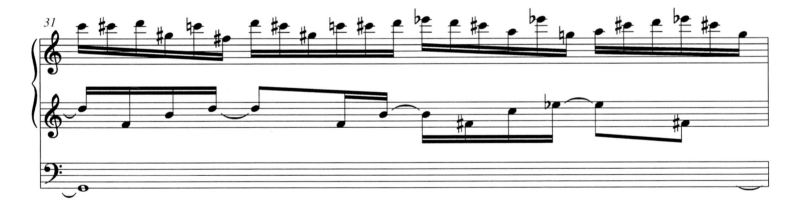

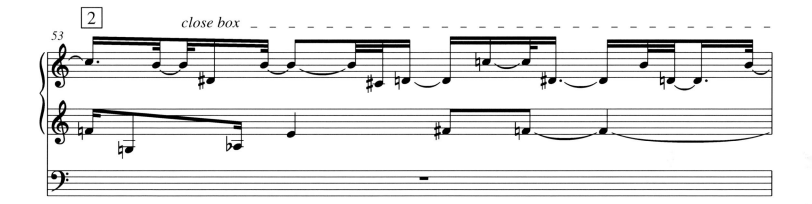

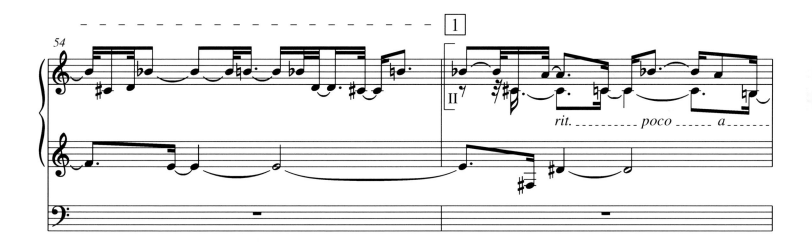

March 29, 1991
Good Friday

M-051-23478-3